Carlota Caulfield

The Book of Giulio Camillo
El Libro de Giulio Camillo
Il Libro di Giulio Camillo

Other Poetry Books by Carlota Caulfield

Fanaim (1984)
Oscuridad divina (1985, 1987)
*A veces me llamo infancia /
Sometimes I Call Myself Childhood* (1985)
El tiempo es una mujer que espera (1986)
34th Street and other poems (1987)
Angel Dust / Polvo de Angel / Polvere d'Angelo (1990)
Estrofas de papel, barro y tinta (1995)
A las puertas del papel con amoroso fuego (1996)
Libro de los XXXIX escalones / Book of the XXXIX Steps (1997)
*Book of the XXXIX Steps: A Poetry Game
of Discovery and Imagination.* CD-ROM (1999)
Quincunce (2001)
Autorretrato en ojo ajeno (2001)
At The Paper Gates With Burning Desire (2001)

Carlota Caulfield

The Book of Giulio Camillo
(a model for a theater of memory)
Translated by Mary G. Berg in collaboration with the author

El Libro de Giulio Camillo
(maqueta para un teatro de la memoria)

Il Libro di Giulio Camillo
(modello per un teatro della memoria)
Traduzione di Pietro Civitareale

Eboli Poetry
An Imprint of InteliBooks *Publishers*

Spanish Language Copyright © 2003 by Carlota Caulfield.
English translation Copyright © 2002 by Mary G. Berg.
Italian translation Copyright © 2002 by Pietro Civitareale.

Cover Design: Damion Gordon - BTP Graphx.
Cover illustration: "A Sort of Dialogue" by Gladys Triana.
Cover photo of the Author by Servando González.

No part of this book may be reproduced or transmitted in any form or by any means, graphic, electronic or mechanical, including photocopying, recording, taping or by any information storage or retrieval system, without permission in writing from the publisher, except by a reviewer, who may quote short passages in a review.

ISBN 0-9711391-4-8 (softcover)

This book was printed in the United States of America
To order additional copies of this book, contact:

InteliBooks
www.InteliBooks.com
Orders@InteliBooks.com

Acknowledgments are made to the editors of the following publications, where some of these poems first appeared:

- *La Intercontinental Poética*. Revista-archivo internacional de poesía contemporánea, Buenos Aires.

- *Las poetas de la búsqueda*. Antología. Editado por Jaime D. Parra (Zaragoza: Libros del Innombrable, 2002).

For Amach,
in memoriam

Contents

Entering Carlota Caulfield's Theatre of Memory,
by John Goodby   xv

The Book of Giulio Camillo   21

El Libro de Giulio Camillo   45

Il Libro di Giulio Camillo   69

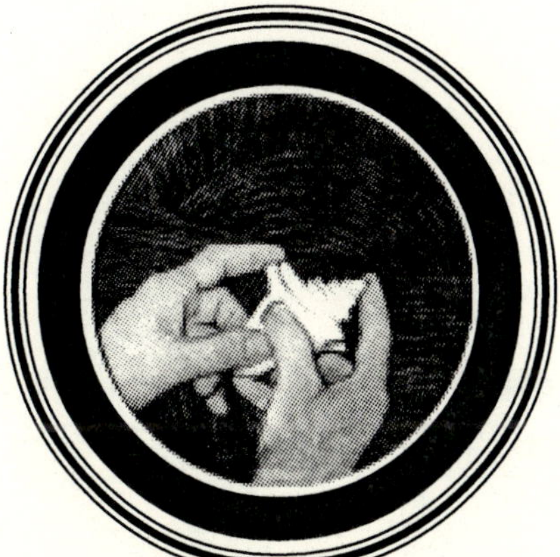

Entering Carlota Caulfield's Theatre of Memory

Carlota Caulfield's project of reclamation of neglected, and sometimes not so neglected lives continues in her *The Book of Giulio Camillo / El Libro de Giulio Camillo / Il Libro di Giulio Camillo.* As her "Note in Homage" informs us, Camillo was one of the most famous men of the Italian Renaissance, renowned for the invention of a "theatre of memory" into which a single spectator would insert his head, to be presented with a view from the stage, as it were, of seven rows of spectators'seats. "It included," Caulfield's note continues, "all branches of knowledge and a method to memorize them as the 'full wisdom of the universe' was presented in 'seven times seven doorways.'" This strange and haunting apparatus, sounding to us like a cross between a virtual reality headset and an image out of de Chirico, is translated into the medium of verse by Caulfield's sevenfold sections of seven tercets which enact, rather than describe, Camillo's theatre. In limpid and piercing verses, Caulfield (superbly served here by her translators, Mary G. Berg and Pietro Civitareale) moves her narrating voice — detached in the manner of Beckett or Borges — from an initial state of desiccated receptivity through the several senses and elements as defined by Renaissance cosmology, to a point of plenitude from which it collapses back into the opening phrase, but changed from a "voiceless mouth" to one which "remains warm."

As ever in Caulfield's work there is an insistence upon the body both as physical presence and as a mode of knowledge, although this is not set against the intellect in any crude anti-rationalist manner. Indeed, the materiality of the world suggested is counter-pointed to moving effect by the clarity and detachment of the language. This, for example, is the point – section IV – at which the "inner beings" in the guise of animals emerge into the theatre:

I
NOR SUCH A FAREWELL
nor such gazing
only thus

II
INNER BEING WHO SWEATS
tricorned trotting beast
intellect, will and memory

III
ABSOLUTE SOUND OF A GOAT'S HORN
marked by water and the story of my back
loving hand that prolongs its breath

IV
TREMBLING AND RESTIVE MEMORY
crossing spaces barefoot
that are not its own

xvi

V
THE LAST CRUST OF BREAD
marked by addicted hands
in the theater of memory

VI
THERE IS A SINGLE SPECTATOR
and no matter how many boxes and drawers he opens
he will not find solace

VII
WITH INSISTENT FURY I SHOUT
to that gaze
that must be made into a bridge

The section illustrates many of the virtues of the poem, and its English translation. There is, for example, the careful uncertainty, the scruple if you like, which refuses to clarify the nature — inner or outer — of its reality; the effect being that we inhabit a kind of meditative limbo which is both urgently attentive and supremely relaxed. Here memory is "barefoot," not merely a cerebral quality; and, despite the impression of a language which has been purged of idiosyncrasy, a second reading reveals stubborn lexical usages — "tricorned," "addicted" — which bear witness to genuine thought, and to its struggle through language to find expression. This aspect, of the inextricability of body and spirit, hints at the roots of memory itself in their conflicting urges, and the whole poem is shot through with a desire which makes it, at one level, a love poem of a pure and metaphysical kind which is rare in English (there is something Marvellian about the images of poise — "Torch blazing on the tip of memory" — and the corresponding equilibrium of the language, which is maintained throughout). Desire roams ceaselessly, is ultimately insatiable, but its voracity may be stayed temporarily in fugitive reference and a hinted-at community ("an urban childhood of dawn stars," "cloth woven with names of cities"), before hurrying on again. This is a ritualistic poem — it rings with echoes of divinatory rites, and abounds with enumerations — but it is resolutely secular, simultaneously erotic and haunted by loss and fragility. The effort it cost Carlota Caulfield may be gauged from the undemonstrative but eloquent dates of composition which conclude the piece — "June 23, 1995" to "June, 1999" — and one can understand why. It is marvelous, yet not an easy work, compelling the reader as it does to confront the theatre of his or her own memories, to "meditate with pure water from mouth to ear" until the memory of some other falls "like warm paper onto warm paper," briefly escaping the prison of the self, of subjectivity, "and so the poem is written."

—John Goodby, University of Wales, Swansea.

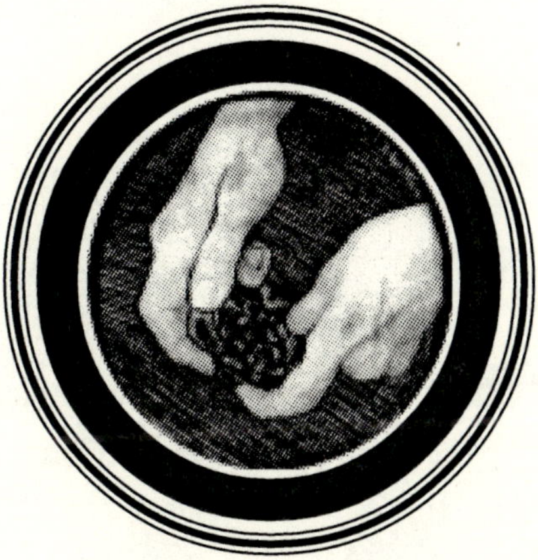

The Book of Giulio Camillo
(a model for a theater of memory)

Translated by Mary G. Berg
in collaboration with the author

NOTE IN HOMAGE

Giulio Camillo Delminio (1480-1544) was one of the most famous men of the Italian Renaissance. He was renowned for his invention of a "theater of memory." His "theater," consisted of a model amphitheater into which a single spectator would insert his head and gaze not toward a stage, but toward the amphitheater's seven rows of spectators' seats. It included all branches of knowledge and a method to memorize them. From the perspective of the stage, the spectator contemplated the full wisdom of the universe which presented itself in seven times seven doorways arranged on the seven ascending levels. The true actors in this spectacle were Wisdom, the Planets and Mythological Beings depicted on small cards placed on the seven levels. Camillo considered that the study of his theater offered the possibility of discovering all the corners of the human soul and of reaching the inmost depths of the mind.

*I am the only spectator of this street.
If I were to stop looking at it, it would disappear.*

Jorge Luis Borges

I

I
THE MEMORY WHICH BEGAN TO TRANSMIT SIGNALS
was the size of a droplet,
and its voiceless mouth remained warm

II
YESTERDAY I WAS A WORDLESS BROKEN URN
a vessel without song, without joy,
with parched skin upon the threshold

III
THE WATER IN THE NIGHT CALLED MY NAME
my right eye open and I was silenced
and suspicious upon gazing so far

IV
FIRST SECOND AND THIRD VOICE
that of those primitive waters
emanating from the air

V
THEY ESTABLISHED THEIR POWERS
and combined the oblique points
and fixed them in five sites in the mouth

VI
NOT TO BE CLEANSED WITH WATER
neither memory nor the tattooed body
the internal marks grope their way

VII
I MEDITATE WITH PURE WATER FROM MOUTH TO EAR
an oblivion that leaves no image
a memory with no audience

II

I
IN SWIFT FLOWING WATER I WRITE
the banquet of silence: water
I taste the flavors of vision: memory

II
YOUR MOUTH WAS ONLY MEMORY
and your tongue dispersed its energy against the wall,
it raced at your bidding, it humbled itself before your throne

III
LATER THE WATER BECAME REDEMPTIVE
it sculpted itself into newly made pillars
waiting for more prudence, less terror

IV
MEMORY IS ALSO GOOD
when it overflows
when it rises up without supplication

V
AND THEY READ MY MEMORY DRAWN FROM MY BONES
and they burned it to divine
like a sacred wound in a sacred vessel

VI
MEMORY WAS BRIEF
and the memory of the memory itself
allowed the hand to retain the word

VII
I DON'T KNOW WHETHER I TOUCHED IT
interlaced threads or texture
cloth woven with names of cities

III

I
MEMORY CONVERTED INTO MESSENGER OF BREATHS
of memory turned to saliva in many mouths,
of memory become a multitude of eyes

II
VISUAL EYE IS THE MIND'S EYE
backstage
prime matter is mixed

III
IN ORDER TO RAISE THE SEVEN PILLARS
which memory asks of wisdom,
reminiscence is simple gaze

IV
MEMORY AND HAND EMBRACING
beneath the water's threshold
and the bird's flight

V
PREMONITION THAT YEARNS FOR FLIGHT
from a silence that hears
the sigh of air

VI
WHISTLING LIKE FIRE, SKIN
couples with a heliotrope
within the sky's view

VII
TO GRASP AND TO RETAIN ARE TWO POWERS
of being: memory
of crossing: hand

IV

I
NOR SUCH A FAREWELL
nor such gazing
only thus

II
INNER BEING WHO SWEATS
tricorned trotting beast
intellect, will and memory

III
ABSOLUTE SOUND OF A GOAT'S HORN
marked by water and the story of my back
loving hand that prolongs its breath

IV
TREMBLING AND RESTIVE MEMORY
crossing spaces barefoot
that are not its own

V
THE LAST CRUST OF BREAD
marked by addicted hands
in the theater of memory

VI
THERE IS A SINGLE SPECTATOR
and no matter how many boxes and drawers he opens
he will not find solace

VII
WITH INSISTENT FURY I SHOUT
to that gaze
that must be made into a bridge

V

I
MEMORY PREPARES TO TAKE FLIGHT
and shrinks its scars, damps its odor
to each his own seamy side

II
MY HISTORIC SUIT IS MADE OF IDENTICAL THREADS
it appreciates the anxiety of my skin
its dream of winged sandals

III
MEMORY AWAKES ON OFFICIAL PAPER
stamped with errant seals and elegant lettering,
vestige of all inner vision, pure touch

IV
THERE: MEANS THE CITY OF AMPHITHEATRES
here: means the city of itineraries,
my here and my there validate each other: destiny

V
TOTALITY AND VOID
and the living creatures
ran and returned

VI
INFINITE THREAD OF SALIVA THAT COMES BACK
to impress upon memory
the absolute eye of the abrupt

VII
LIKE A SACRED SEED THE HAND FEELS
an urban childhood of dawn stars
and words of warm densities

VI

I
THE INSTANT'S TOUCH FINDS
a hand that opens words
in a time no longer distant

II
AND THE MIND'S TRACE
is defined in seeds filled with water:
dark and sacred music

III
WITH HUNGRY RITE THE BODY ASCENDS
to its traces in another's eye,
to be wounded in its own self

IV
UNDER THE WORD OF THE EYE'S PUPIL TO THE BODY
in a crossing that spins images
voices of all the memories

V
MEMORY OF THE OBJECT
breeds thirst
while sounds break out

VI
OF ALL THE UNKNOWN VOICES
there is only one I manage to name
and hear

VII
THE SOUL COMES LOOKING FOR YOU
body breaking up in total love,
so that memory may drink

VII

I
TORCH BLAZING ON THE TIP OF MEMORY
with fresh clothing that ignores the dead
and a perverse slowness

II
THE WATCHFUL EYE TRAVELS CALMLY
through the wise doorways, it says,
and who deciphers the inner script?

III
THE TEMPLE IS CALLED A THEATER
and with pillars of intellect and love
constructs a power called memory

IV
YOUR MEMORY FALLS UPON MY MEMORY
like warm paper onto warm paper,
and so the poem is written

V
AIR, FIRE AND WATER
are round creatures,
a triad that can be anything

VI
THE ARTS OF MEMORY
hide themselves in you in vain,
your memory

VII
THE MEMORY WHICH BEGAN TO TRANSMIT SIGNALS
was the size of a droplet,
and its voiceless mouth remained warm

The Book of Giulio Camillo was begun in Barcelona on June 23, 1995, continued in San Sebastián in July of that year, and finished in Paris in June, 1999.

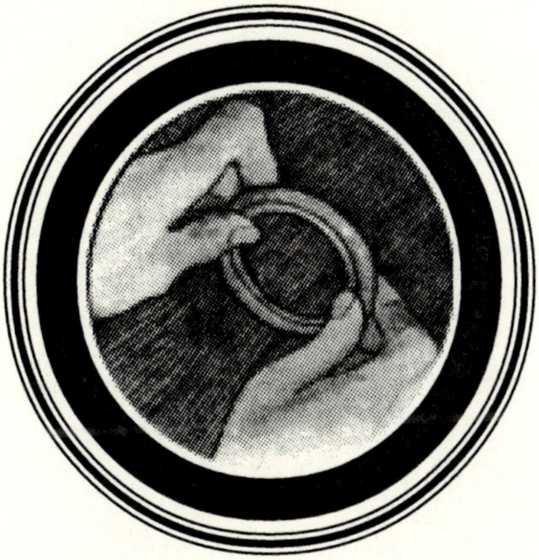

El Libro de Giulio Camillo
(maqueta para un teatro de la memoria)

NOTA-HOMENAJE

Giulio Camillo Delminio (1480-1544) fue uno de los hombres más famosos del Renacimiento italiano. Su notoriedad se debió a la invención de su "teatro de la memoria". En su "teatro", que consistía en una maqueta en la que el espectador único introducía la cabeza y miraba no hacia el escenario, sino hacia las gradas, acomodó todas las ramas del conocimiento y la manera de memorizarlas. Desde el escenario, el espectador contemplaba toda la sabiduría del universo que se presentaba en siete veces siete puertas colocadas en siete gradas ascendentes. Los verdaderos actores de este espectáculo eran la sabiduría, los planetas y los seres mitológicos representados en pequeñas tarjetas colocadas en las gradas. Camillo consideraba que el estudio de su teatro daba la posibilidad de conocer todos los rincones del alma humana y de llegar a lo más recóndito de la mente.

Yo soy el único espectador de esta calle,
Si dejara de verla, se moriría.

Jorge Luis Borges

I

I
DEL TAMAÑO DE UNA GOTA FUE LA MEMORIA
que empezó a transmitir señales,
y la boca quedó tibia sin voz

II
AYER FUI CÁNTARO DESTROZADO SIN PALABRA
vasija sin canto, sin júbilo,
con piel seca a la entrada de la casa

III
EL AGUA EN LA NOCHE ME NOMBRABA,
abierto el ojo derecho me hizo muda
y sospechosa por mirar tan lejos

IV
VOZ PRIMERA, SEGUNDA Y TERCERA
la de aquellas aguas primitivas
que emanan del aire

V
ESTABLECIERON LOS PODERES
y combinaron los puntos oblicuos
y los fijaron en cinco lugares de la boca

VI
NO SE LIMPIA CON AGUA
ni la memoria ni el cuerpo tatuado,
las marcas internas andan a tientas

VII
REFLEXIONO CON AGUA FINA DE LA BOCA AL OÍDO
un olvido que no deja imagen,
una memoria que no tiene público

II

I
ESCRIBO EN AGUA RÁPIDA
el banquete de la mudez: agua
pruebo los sabores de la visión: memoria

II
MEMORIA SÓLO FUE TU BOCA
y la lengua dispersó su fuerza contra el muro,
corrió por su mandato, se humilló ante su trono

III
DESPUÉS EL AGUA SE HIZO REDENTORA
se esculpió en pilares frescos,
esperando más prudencia, menos terror

IV
LA MEMORIA TAMBIÉN ES BUENA
cuando se derrama,
cuando se alza sin súplicas

V
Y LEYERON MI MEMORIA SALIDA DE LOS HUESOS
y la quemaron para adivinar
como herida sagrada en sagrado vaso

VI
FUE CORTA LA MEMORIA
y el recuerdo del recuerdo mismo
dejó que la mano retuviera la palabra

VII
NO SÉ SI PUDE TOCARLA
tejido o textura,
tela urdida con nombres de ciudades

III

I
MEMORIA CONVERTIDA EN MENSAJERA DE ALIENTOS
de memoria hecha saliva en muchas bocas,
de memoria vuelta multitud de ojos

II
OJO VISUAL ES EL OJO DE LA MENTE
detrás del escenario
la materia prima se mezcla

III
PARA ALZAR LOS SIETE PILARES
que la memoria le pide a la sabiduría,
la reminiscencia es simple mirada

IV
MEMORIA Y MANO ABRAZADAS
bajo el umbral del agua
y el vuelo del pájaro

V
PRESAGIO QUE SE AFANA AL VUELO
de una mudez que oye
el hálito del aire

VI
SIBILANTE COMO EL FUEGO LA PIEL
se acopla con un heliotropo
que está a la mira del cielo

VII
ASIR Y RETENER SON DOS PODERES
de la estancia: memoria
de la travesía: mano

IV

I
NI TANTA DESPEDIDA
ni tanto mirar,
sólo así

II
SER INTERIOR QUE SUDA
animal tricornio de trote,
intelecto, voluntad y memoria

III
SONIDO ABSOLUTO DEL CUERNO DE CABRA
marcado por el agua y la historia de mi espalda,
mano amante que prolonga su aliento

IV
MEMORIA TEMBLOROSA Y VIAJERA
que descalza cruza espacios
que no le pertenecen

V
EL ÚLTIMO PEDAZO DE PAN
marcado por adictas manos
en el teatro de la memoria

VI
HAY UN SOLO ESPECTADOR
y por más cajas y gavetas que abra
no encontrará holgura

VII
CON RABIA EXIGENTE GRITO
a esa mirada
hay que hacerla puente

V

I
LA MEMORIA SE DISPONE A EMPRENDER VUELO
y hace livianas sus cicatrices, apaga su olor,
a cada cual su piel de hilachas

II
DE IDÉNTICOS HILOS ES MI TRAJE HISTÓRICO
que agradece la zozobra en la piel,
su sueño de sandalias aladas

III
LA MEMORIA SE DESPIERTA EN PAPEL TIMBRADO
con matasellos vagabundo y letra de pluma fina,
despojo de toda visión interior, puro tacto

IV
ALLÍ, SIGNIFICA LA CIUDAD DE LOS ANFITEATROS
aquí, significa la ciudad de los itinerarios,
mi allí y mi aquí se validan: destino

V
LA TOTALIDAD Y EL VACÍO
y las criaturas vivientes
corrieron y volvieron

VI
INFINITO HILO DE SALIVA QUE REGRESA
a imprimir en la memoria
el ojo absoluto de lo súbito

VII
COMO SEMILLA SAGRADA LA MANO PALPA
una niñez urbana de madrugadas estrellas
y palabras de tibias espesuras

VI

I
TACTO DEL INSTANTE QUE ENCUENTRA
una mano que abre vocablos
en un tiempo en que lo lejano ya no es

II
Y EL TRAZO DE LA MENTE
se define en semillas llenas de agua:
música oscura y sagrada

III
CON HAMBRIENTO RITUAL ASCIENDE EL CUERPO
a su huella en ojo ajeno,
ser herido en sí mismo

IV
BAJA LA PALABRA DE LA PUPILA AL CUERPO
en travesía que hilvana figuras,
voces de todos los recuerdos

V
LA MEMORIA DEL OBJETO
engendra sed,
mientras estalla en rumores

VI
DE TODAS LAS VOCES DESCONOCIDAS
hay una sola que consigo nombrar,
y escucho

VII
LLEGA EL ALMA A BUSCARTE
cuerpo quebrantado en todo amor,
para que la memoria beba

VII

I
ANTORCHA PRENDIDA EN LA PUNTA DE LA MEMORIA
con ropa fresca que ignora a los muertos,
y una perversa lentitud

II
EL OJO CUIDADOR VIAJA TRANQUILO
por las puertas sabias, dice,
¿y quién descifra la taquigrafía interior?

III
EL TEMPLO SE LLAMA TEATRO
y con pilares de intelecto y de amor
construye una energía llamada memoria

IV
TU MEMORIA CAE SOBRE MI MEMORIA
como papel tibio sobre papel tibio,
y así queda escrito el poema

V
AIRE, FUEGO Y AGUA
son criaturas redondas,
tríada que puede ser cualquier cosa

VI
LAS ARTES DE LA MEMORIA
en vano se ocultan en ti,
memoria tuya

VII
DEL TAMAÑO DE UNA GOTA FUE LA MEMORIA
que empezó a transmitir señales,
y la boca quedó tibia sin voz

El libro de Giulio Camillo empezó a escribirse en Barcelona el 23 de junio de 1995, creció en San Sebastián en julio, y fue terminado en París en junio de 1999.

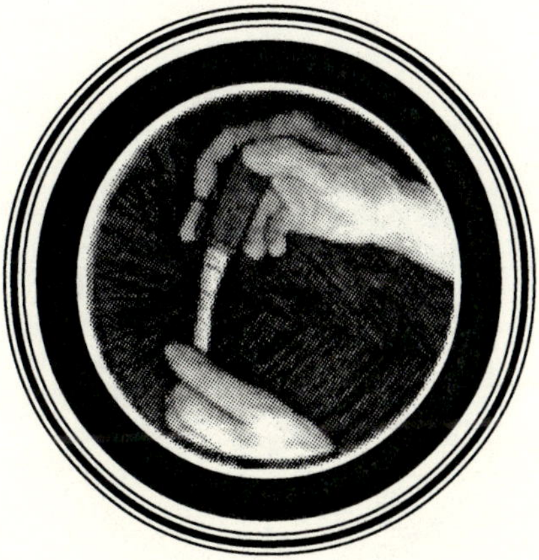

Il Libro di Giulio Camillo
(modello per un teatro della memoria)
Traduzione di Pietro Civitareale

NOTA-OMAGGIO

Giulio Camillo Delminio (1490-1544) fu uno degli uomini più famosi del Rinascimento italiano. La sua notorietà è dovuta all'invenzione del "Teatro della memoria". Nel suo "Teatro", che consisteva in un modello architettonico in forma di teatro nel quale un singolo spettatore introduceva la testa e guardava non verso lo scenario ma verso le gradinate, sistemò tutti i rami della conoscenza e la maniera di memorizzarla. Da una simile prospettiva lo spettatore contemplava tutto il sapere dell'universo ripartito sette volte, in sette porte collocate su sette livelli di gradini ascendenti. I veri attori di questo spettacolo erano la sapienza, i pianeti e gli esseri mitologici rappresentati su piccole targhette piazzate sulle gradinate. Camillo riteneva che lo studio del suo "teatro" offriva la possibilità di conoscere tutti gli angoli dell'anima e di giungere nelle profondità più segrete della mente.

*Io sono l'unico spettatore di questa via,
Se smettessi di vederla morirei.*

Jorge Luis Borges

I

I
DALLA GRANDEZZA D'UNA GOCCIA LA MEMORIA
incominciò a trasmettere segnali,
e la bocca si fece tiepida, senza voce

II
IERI SONO STATA ANFORA SPEZZATA PRIVA DI PAROLA,
vaso senza canto, senza allegria,
con pelle secca nell'atrio della casa

III
L'ACQUA NELLA NOTTE MI NOMINAVA
l'occhio destro aperto mi rese muta
e sospettosa per guardare così lontano

IV
PRIMA VOCE, SECONDA E TERZA
quella delle acque primordiali
che procedono dall'aria

V
STABILIRONO I POTERI
ed accordarono i punti obliqui,
fissandoli in cinque luoghi della bocca

VI
NON SI PURIFICA CON L'ACQUA
né la memoria né il corpo tatuato,
i segnali interni vanno a caso

VII
MEDITO CON ACQUA PURA DALLA BOCCA ALL'ORECCHIO
una dimenticanza che non lascia traccia,
una memoria che non ha pubblico

II

I
SCRIVO SU ACQUA CORRENTE
il banchetto della mutezza: acqua
provo i sapori della visione: memoria

II
SOLTANTO MEMORIA È STATA LA TUA BOCCA
e la lingua ha disperso la sua forza contro il muro,
ha corso per suo ordine, si è umiliata dinanzi al suo trono

III
POI L'ACQUA SI È FATTA RIGENERATRICE,
si è incisa su pilastri appeni eretti,
in attesa d'una maggiore prudenza, di un minor terrore

IV
ANCHE LA MEMORIA È UTILE
quando si prodiga,
quando si alza orgogliosa

V
E LESSERO LA MIA MEMORIA USCITA DALLE OSSA
e la bruciarono per fare predizioni
come ferita sacra in sacro vaso

VI
È STATA CORTA LA MEMORIA
e il ricordo dello stesso ricordo
ha lasciato che la mano trattenesse la parola

VII
NON SO SE POTEI TOCCARLA
tessuto o tessitura,
tela ordita con nomi di città

III

I
MEMORIA CONVERTITA IN MESSAGGERA DI RESPIRI
di memoria fatta saliva in molte bocche,
di memoria diventata folla d'occhi

II
E'OCCHIO VISUALE L'OCCHIO DELLA MENTE
dietro lo scenario
la materia prima si mescola

III
PER ERIGERE I SETTE PILASTRI
che la memoria chiede alla saggezza,
la riminiscenza è semplice sguardo

IV
MEMORIA E MANO AVVINGHIATE
sotto la soglia dell'acqua
e il volo dell'uccello

V
PRESAGIO CHE SI AFFANNA AL VOLO
d'una mutezza che sente
l'alito dell'aria

VI
SIBILANTE COME IL FUOCO LA PELLE
si accoppia con un girasole
che sta sorvegliando il cielo

VII
PRENDERE E TRATTENERE SONO DUE POTERI
dell'essere: memoria
della traversata: mano

IV

I
NÈ COMMIATO
né sguardo,
solo così

II
ESSERE INTERIORE CHE TRASUDA,
trottante animale tricorne,
intelletto, volontà e memoria

III
SUONO ASSOLUTO DEL CORNO CAPRINO,
marcato dall'acqua e dalla storia della mia schiena,
mano amante che prolunga il suo respiro

IV
MEMORIA TREPIDANTE E VAGABONDA
che incrocia, scalza, spazi
che non le appartengono

V
L'ULTIMO PEZZO DI PANE
segnato da mani fedeli
nel teatro della memoria

VI
C'È UN SOLO SPETTATORE
e per quanto apra casse e cassetti
non troverà conforto

VII
CON RABBIA INSISTENTE IO GRIDO
allo sguardo
la necessità di farlo ponte

V

I
LA MEMORIA SI PREPARA A PRENDERE IL VOLO
e fa più leggere le sue cicatrici, spegne il suo odore,
a ciascuno la sua pelle sfilacciata

II
DEGLI STESSI FILI È FATTO IL MIO VESTITO STORICO
che ringrazia l'apprensione della mia pelle,
il suo sogno di sandali alati

III
LA MEMORIA SI DESTA SULLA CARTA BOLLATA
con sigilli vagabondi e lettera di penna fine,
spoglia di tutte le visioni interiori, puro tatto

IV
LÌ VUOL DIRE LA CITTÀ DEGLI ANFITEATRI
qui, vuol dire la città degli itinerari,
il mio lì e il mio qui si confermano a vicenda: destino

V
LA TOTALITÀ E IL VUOTO
e le creature viventi
corsero e ritornarono

VI
INFINITO FILO DI SALIVA CHE RITORNA
a imprimere nella memoria
l'occhio assoluto dell' inaspettato

VII
COMO SEME SACRO LA MANO PALPA
una infanzia urbana di sollecite stelle
e parole di tiepidi spessori

VI

I
TATTO ISTANTANEO CHE TROVA
una mano che apre vocaboli
in un tempo in cui non esiste più distanza

II
E IL TRACCIATO DELLA MENTE
si definisce in semi pieni d'acqua:
musica oscura e sacra

III
CON FAMELICO RITO IL CORPO ASCENDE
sulla sua orma in un occhio alieno,
essere ferito in se stesso

IV
ABBASSA LA PAROLA DALLA PUPILLA AL CORPO
in una traversata che imbastisce figure
voci d'ogni ricordo

V
LA MEMORIA DELL'OGGETTO
che genera sete,
mentre scoppia in suoni

VI
D'OGNI VOCE SCONOSCIUTA
ve n'è solo una che intendo nominare
ed ascolto

VII
L'ANIMA GIUNGE A CERCARTI
corpo spezzato in un amore totale
perché la memoria beva

VII

I
TORCIA ACCESA SULLA PUNTA DELLA MEMORIA
con tessuto leggero che ignora i morti,
ed una perversa lentezza

II
L'OCCHIO METICOLOSO VIAGGIA TRANQUILO
attraverso sagge porte, dice,
e chi decifra la scrittura interiore?

III
IL TEMPLO È CHIAMATO TEATRO
e con pilastri di ingegno ed amore
costruisce una energia chiamata memoria

IV
LA TUA MEMORIA CADE SULLA MIA MEMORIA
come tiepida carta su tiepida carta
e così il poema è scritto

V
ARIA, FUOCO ED ACQUA
sono creature rotonde,
triade che può essere qualsiasi cosa

VI

LE ARTI DELLA MEMORIA
invano si celano in te,
memoria tua

VII
DALLA GRANDEZZA D'UNA GOCCIA LA MEMORIA
incominciò a trasmettere segnali,
e la bocca si fece tiepida, senza voce

Il Libro di Giulio Camillo fu iniziato a Barcelona il 23 giugno del 1995, fu continuato a San Sebastiano in luglio ed è stato terminato a Parigi nel giugno del 1999.

About the Author

CARLOTA CAULFIELD was born in Havana, Cuba. She is the author of *Fanaim* (1984), *Oscuridad divina* (1985 & 1987), *A veces me llamo infancia/Sometimes I call myself childhood* (1985), *El tiempo es una mujer que espera* (1986), *34th Street & other poems* (1987), *Angel Dust/Polvo de Angel/Polvere D'Angelo* (1990), *Libro de los XXXIX escalones/Libro dei XXXIX gradini* (1995), *Estrofas de papel, barro y tinta* (1995), *Libro de los XXXIX escalones/ Book of the XXXIX Steps* (1997), *A las puertas del papel con amoroso fuego* (1996), *Book of the XXXIX Steps, a poetry game of discovery and imagination*, CD-ROM (1999), *Quincunce* (2001), *Autorretrato en ojo ajeno* (2001) and *At the Paper Gates with Burning Desire* (2001).

Her work has appeared, among others, in *Haight Ashbury Literary Journal, Michigan Quarterly Review, Poetry San Francisco, Visions, Beacons, Turia, The Texas Review, Barcarola, Nómada, Cuadernos del Matemático, Aleph, AErea, Tercer Milenio,* and *Chasqui*. Among the poetry prizes she has won are the International poetry prize, "Ultimo Novecento," in Italy (1988), Honorable Mention at the "Plural Prize" of Mexico City (1993), the Honorable Mention in the International Poetry Prize "Federico García

Lorca," (Spain-USA-1994), the International Poetry Prize "Riccardo Marchi-Torre di Calafuria," in Italy, (1995), the 1997 Latino Literature Prize Honorable Mention of the Latin American Writers Institute of New York, and the First Hispanic-American poetry prize "Dulce María Loynaz" (2002).

Her poetry page is at:
http://www.intelinet.org.Caulfield

Nota sobre la autora

CARLOTA CAULFIELD nació en La Habana, Cuba. Es autora de *Fanaim* (1984), *Oscuridad divina* (1985 & 1987), *A veces me llamo infancia/Sometimes I call myself childhood* (1985), *El tiempo es una mujer que espera* (1986), *34th Street & other poems* (1987), *Angel Dust/Polvo de Angel/Polvere D'Angelo* (1990), *Libro de los XXXIX escalones/Libro dei XXXIX gradini* (1995), *Estrofas de papel, barro y tinta* (1995), *Libro de los XXXIX escalones/Book of the XXXIX Steps* (1997), *A las puertas del papel con amoroso fuego* (1996), *Book of the XXXIX Steps, a poetry game of discovery and imagination*, CDRom (1999), *Quincunce* (2001), *Autorretrato en ojo ajeno* (2001) y *At the Paper Gates with Burning Desire* (2001).

Sus poemas han sido publicados en numerosas revistas literarias, entre las que se encuentran *Haight Ashbury Literary Journal, Michigan Quarterly Review, Poetry San Francisco, Visions, Beacons, Turia, The Texas Review, Barcarola, Nómada, Cuadernos del Matemático, Aleph, AErea, Tercer Milenio, y Chasqui*. Entre los premios que su obra ha recibido se encuentran el Premio Internacional "Ultimo Novecento" (Italia, 1988), Mención de Honor en el "Premio Plural" (México, 1992), Mención de Honor en el Premio

Internacional "Federico García Lorca" (Estados Unidos-España, 1994), Premio Internacional "Riccardo Marchi-Torre di Calafuria" (Italia, 1995), Mención de Honor en el "Latino Literature Prize" del Instituto de escritores latinoamericanos de New York (1997), y el Primer Premio Hispanoamericano de poesía "Dulce María Loynaz" (2002).

Su página de poesía en la red puede verse en:
http://www.intelinet.org.Caulfield

Nota sull'autrice

CARLOTA CAULFIELD è nata nell'Avana, Cuba. Ha pubblicato: *Fanaim* (1984), *Oscuridad divina* (1985 & 1987), *A veces me llamo infancia/Sometimes I call myself childhood* (1985), *El tiempo es una mujer que espera* (1986), *34th Street & other poems* (1987), *Angel Dust/Polvo de Angel/Polvere D'Angelo* (1990), *Libro de los XXXIX escalones/Libro dei XXXIX gradini* (1995), *Estrofas de papel, barro y tinta* (1995), *Libro de los XXXIX escalones/ Book of the XXXIX Steps* (1997), *A las puertas del papel con amoroso fuego* (1996), *Book of the XXXIX Steps, a poetry game of discovery and imagination*, CDRom (1999), *Quincunce* (2001), *Autorretrato en ojo ajeno* (2001) e *At the Paper Gates with Burning Desire* (2001).

Suoi versi sono stati pubblicati in numerose riviste letterarie, tra le quali: *Haight Ashbury Literary Journal, Michigan Quarterly Review, Poetry San Francisco, Visions, Beacons, Turia, The Texas Review, Barcarola, Nómada, Cuadernos del Matemático, Aleph, AErea, Tercer Milenio,* e *Chasqui*. Tra i premi ricevuti vanno menzionati: Premio Internazionale di poesia "Pisa – Ultimo Novecento" (Italia, 1988), "Menzione d'onore" al "Premio Plural"(Messico, 1993) "Menzione d'onore" al Premio Internazionale

"Federico García Lorca," (Stati Uniti-Spagna, 1994), Premio Internazionale "Riccardo Marchi-Torre di Calafuria," (Italia, 1995), la "Menzione d'onore" "Latino Literature Prize" dell'Istituto di scrittori latinoamericani di New York (1997), e il Premio di poesia "Dulce María Loynaz" (2002).

La sua pagina di poesia si trova in:
http://www.intelinet.org.Caulfield

About the Translators

MARY G. BERG grew up in Colombia and Peru. She has written extensively about Latin American women writers, and has translated works by Angélica Gorodischer, Ana María Shúa, Clorinda Matto, Juana Manuela Gorriti, Marjorie Agosin, Laura Riesco y Carlota Caulfield. Her most recent translated book is Libertad Demitrópulos' *River of Sorrows* published by White Pine Press. She currently teaches in Harvard University's Extension program.

PIETRO CIVITAREALE è nato e cresciuto in Italia. Come poeta ha all'attivo una decina di volumi di versi in lingua e in dialetto abruzzese (*Un modo di essere*, 1983; *Il fumo degli anni,* 1989; *Solitudine delle parole,* 1995; *La miele de ju mmierne,* 1998; *Ombre disegnate,* 2001); come saggista, si è occupato di D. Valeri, C. Betocchi, F. Fortini, V. Clemente, E. Montale, R. Baldini, J. Joyce, S. Beckett, G. Grass, R. Musil, F. Garcia Lorca e di alcuni aspetti dell' arte contemporanea; come traduttore ha curato, tra l'altro, un'antologia delle poesie di F. Pessoa (*L' enigma e le maschere,* 1993 e 1996) ed un'edizione parziale delle *Novelle esemplari* di Miguel de Cervantes (1998). È del 2002 la pubblicazione di una raccolta di racconti, ispirati all'Abruzzo, intitolata *Vecchie storie.*

About the Cover Artist

GLADYS TRIANA was born in Camagüey, Cuba. She lived in Spain from 1969 to 1975. In 1975 she moved to New York, and still resides there. She has worked with different media: painting, drawing, engraving, sculpture, instalations and photography. She has had several personal exhibitions in Havana, Madrid, Paris, Lima, Stockholm, Caracas, Santo Domingo, Miami and New York; and has participated in group exhibitions in Havana, México, Bogotá, Caracas, Belgium, Ireland, Santiago de Chile, Malmo, Otawa, and Buenos Aires. In the U.S. her works have been exhibited in Austin, Washington, Miami, Tampa, Fort Lauderdale, Chicago, Minnesota, Baltimore, Connecticut, Long Beach, California, Albany and other cities.

Triana was the recipient of a Cintas Foundation Fellowship in 1993. Her work has been included in prestigious compilations and encyclopedias of contemporary art: *Memoria: Cuban Art of the Twenty Century* (California International Art Foundation, 2002), *Time Capsule: A Concise Encyclopedia by Women Artists* (New York, 1995), *Lines of Vision: Drawing by Contemporary Women* (New York, 1989), *Art of Cuba in Exile* (Miami, 1987), *Enciclopedia de Cuba* (Miami, 1975), and *Pintores Cubanos* (La Habana: Ediciones R, 1962).

Her work has also appeared in covers and illustrations of books of various contemporary poets and writers, among them Magali Alabau's *Ras* (Santiago de Chile: Ediciones El Maintén, 1986) and *Electra, Clitemnestra* (Santiago de Chile, Ediciones El Maintén, 1987); Felipe Lázaro's *Poetas cubanas en Nueva York* (Madrid: Editorial Betania, 1991); José Triana's, *Teatro* (Madrid: Editorial Verbum, 1991) and *Teatro en un tiempo* (New Jersey: Editorial Ollantay, 1999); and, more recently, Iraida Iturralde's, *La isla rota* (Madrid: Editorial Verbum, 2002). Her illustrations have also appeared important literary magazines, among them, *Escandalar*, *Mariel* and *Linden Lane Magazine*.

Books by Carlota Caulfield
available in the Eboli Poetry series
of InteliBooks:

At the Paper Gates With Burning Desire
(Spansih / English)

Translated by Angela McEwan
in collaboration with the author,
with an Intrduction by Marjorie Agosín

COLOPHON

Type composition for this book was accomplished on a Power Macintosh G3 computer in Goudy Old Style type.

In 1915, Frederic W. Goudy designed Goudy Old Style, his twenty-fifth typeface, and his first for American Type Founders. Flexible enough for both text and display, it is one of the most popular typefaces ever produced. Its recognizable features include the diamond-shaped dots on i, j, and on punctuation marks; the upturned ear of the g; and the base of E and L.

Several years later, in response to the overwhelming popularity of Cooper Black, Lanston Monotype commissioned Frederic W. Goudy to design heavy versions of Goudy Old Style. Goudy Heavyface and Goudy Heavyface Italic were released in 1925. The huge success of Goudy's typefaces led to the addition of several weights to many of his typefaces; designers working for American Type Founders produced additions to the family. In 1927, Morris Fuller Benton drew Goudy Extra Bold.

Printed in the United States
1044300001B/194